This book belongs to:

____

Written by Kim Ivie

Illustrated by Juliana Miller

Dedicated to my kindergartners who
make me smile and laugh every day.
– Miss Ivie

Winter is a glorious time!

There are many matters you may find sublime...

there's sledding!

and skiing...

and also snowmachining!

Yet, when the months near December, there are a few safety things that you need to remember...

Snow gear keeps you warm and snug, so keep it on and stay warm like a hug!

Snow may be bright, fluffy, and white, but...

it 's not clean so don 't dare take a bite!

9

All manner of things walk on the snow, leaving behind all kinds of germs we don't know!

So think to yourself...
The snow stays on the ground,
the snow stays on the ground,
don't eat it, or lick it,
the snow stays on the ground.

When it comes to metal objects in the winter, you will want to reconsider...

Tongues get stuck so don't push your luck!

Snow castles, snow men...

snow angels, snow races...

There's fun of all kinds for kids of all ages!

When near frigid
water or a frozen
lake, remember that it
is wise to stay on land
or the ice may break!

Moose are graceful, lovely and large, but remember this so you don 't get a charge!

Quietly give it some space and go the other way, or run and get cover — just don 't stay!

Snowballs are fun
for home and for
snowdays, but avoid
being cruel and don 't
throw them at school!

home sweet HOME

When playing at home, make sure someone knows where you are. Parents get worried and may begin to search near and far.

And lastly, when playing
at dark, have mom or dad
add reflectives to your
jacket so you'll be bright
like a spark!

Kim Ivie teaches kindergarten in North Pole, Alaska. She is passionate about teaching Kindergarten and seeing her students' excitement as they learn new things and conquer the world. Kim knows how important it is to keep safety in mind while playing outside, and decided to put it all in a book so parents and teachers can help their little ones remember the top winter safety rules.

Juliana Miller is a mom and illustrator living in North Pole, Alaska. She has always had a love for art and is ecstatic she can draw and make art while educating her children at home. She creates most of her artwork digitally, but also enjoys working in oil paints, watercolor, and colored pencils.

She is always looking for fun new projects and can be reached at julesmarionart@gmail.com.